I0814866

WORLD WAR II

WORLD WAR II IN EUROPE

BY JANIE HAVEMEYER

CONTENT CONSULTANT
Phyllis L. Soybel, PhD
Professor, Department of History
College of Lake County

Cover image: Many cities in Europe, including parts of Cologne, Germany, were destroyed during World War II.

Core Library
An Imprint of Abdo Publishing
abdobooks.com

abdobooks.com

Published by Abdo Publishing, a division of ABDO, PO Box 398166, Minneapolis, Minnesota 55439.

Printed in the United States of America, North Mankato, Minnesota.
052024
092024

Cover Photo: Galerie Bilderwelt/Hulton Archive/Getty Images
Interior Photos: Universal History Archive/Universal Images Group/Getty Images, 4–5; Hulton-Deutsch Collection/Corbis Historical/Getty Images, 6, 29; ullstein bild Dtl./Getty Images, 9; Albert Harlingue/Roger Viollet/Getty Images, 12–13; Red Line Editorial, 15, 41; Topical Press Agency/Hulton Archive/Getty Images, 16; Bettmann/Getty Images, 18, 20–21, 36, 45; Crown/Mirrorpix/Getty Images, 22; Keystone-France/Gamma-Keystone/Getty Images, 26–27, 43; Mondadori Portfolio/Getty Images, 34–35

Editor: Marley Richmond
Series Designer: Ryan Gale

Library of Congress Control Number: 2023949024

Publisher's Cataloging-in-Publication Data

Names: Havemeyer, Janie, author.
Title: World war II in Europe / by Janie Havemeyer
Description: Minneapolis, Minnesota: Abdo Publishing, 2025 | Series: World war II | Includes online resources and index.
Identifiers: ISBN 9781098293680 (lib. bdg.) | ISBN 9798384912958 (ebook)
Subjects: LCSH: World War, 1939-1945--Juvenile literature. | Europe--Juvenile literature. | Military campaigns--Juvenile literature. | Armed forces--Juvenile literature. | Politics and government--Juvenile literature.
Classification: DDC 940.53--dc23

CONTENTS

CHAPTER ONE

THE INVASION OF POLAND

Wladyslaw Szpilman woke up to the distant sound of explosions. He turned on his radio. It was September 1, 1939. "Hello. Hello. This is Warsaw on all its wavelengths," the announcer said. "At 5:40 German troops crossed the Polish frontier. . . . A number of cities were bombed." Szpilman lived in Warsaw, the Polish capital. He dressed and rushed outside. Sirens blared from the loudspeakers installed on lampposts, in windows, and over

Throughout September 1939, German soldiers marched into Poland.

In between bombing attacks, Polish people dug trenches throughout Warsaw. Many children helped. These trenches provided shelter during air raids.

shop doorways. "This is an alarm warning for the city of Warsaw. Be on alert!"

All across Poland, German planes howled. Bombs destroyed bridges, railroads, and airfields. People ran and screamed. The Germans were cutting off routes in and out of Warsaw. The city was under siege.

Soldiers marched across the Polish border. Tanks sped through the countryside toward Polish cities. Many were headed to Warsaw. The city was the location of the Polish government. It was an important target. The Germans expected Warsaw to surrender without a fight. But the Poles were determined to defend their capital.

For more than three weeks, Polish citizens watched their city turn into rubble. Churches, museums, and homes were destroyed by bombs. Then in the early afternoon of September 27, there was a sudden silence. Warsaw had surrendered. The Germans had won the battle.

HITLER AND THE PATH TO WAR

Tensions had been rising in Europe since the end of World War I (1914–1918). Many nations blamed Germany for that conflict. The nations that won World War I took parts of Germany's territory and forced the country to pay for damages. Many Germans believed these consequences were unfair.

Shortly after World War I, Adolf Hitler began rising to power in Germany. He took leadership of the Nazi Party and claimed that he would fight back against the harsh punishments Germany faced. But the Nazi Party was also nationalistic and anti-Semitic. Nazis passed anti-Jewish laws and blamed Jews for many of Germany's problems. In 1934 Hitler named himself führer, the head of Germany. He soon became a dictator. Hitler wanted to expand Germany's territory and build a new German empire in Europe.

REICHSTAG SPEECH

On January 30, 1939, Hitler made a speech to the German parliament, which was called the Reichstag. He said that war would mean the end of European Jews. The Nazi genocide of Jewish people had begun. The Nazis spread racist lies to give reasons for killing Jews. They said Jews were dangerous and would not be loyal to Germany.

German forces had already conquered Austria in 1938. They had occupied Bohemia and Moravia earlier in 1939. These were provinces of the Czecho-Slovak state. In August 1939, Hitler made a pact with the Soviet Union

Adolf Hitler made many anti-Semitic claims during his Reichstag Speech on January 30, 1939.

PERSPECTIVES

NOT WAR

Hitler thought that if Germany had a legitimate reason to invade Poland, France and Great Britain might not strike back. So he created a fake reason. German soldiers disguised in Polish uniforms attacked a German radio station. Hitler said Poland had attacked Germany first. German officials were told to say, "German troops moved into action against Poland at dawn today. This action is for the present not to be described as war, but merely as engagements which have been brought about by Polish attacks."

and its leader, Joseph Stalin. This agreement was called the Molotov-Ribbentrop Pact. Germany and the Soviet Union agreed to invade and occupy Poland in September 1939. They also pledged not to attack each other for ten years.

Germany attacked Poland on September 1. Britain and France declared war on Germany two days later. They had promised to protect Poland if it was invaded. Britain and France started an alliance that would become the Allied powers. Stalin waited to see what would happen after Germany invaded Poland. He didn't want to be caught in a war if the German invasion failed. Eventually Stalin thought it was clear Germany would win. He invaded Poland from the east on September 17.

Warsaw surrendered on September 27, 1939. Poland fell soon after. Britain and France had not been able to help in time. Germany and the Soviet Union divided the country. The Soviets got eastern Poland, and Germany took western Poland, which included Warsaw. World War II (1939–1945) had begun, and the fighting would continue for years to come.

EXPLORE ONLINE

Chapter One discusses the German invasion of Poland. The website below explores the invasion and its consequences. What new information did you learn from this website?

INVASION OF POLAND

abdocorelibrary.com/world-war-ii-europe

CHAPTER TWO

THE BATTLE OF FRANCE

After Germany invaded Poland in September 1939, Hitler set his sights on France. France was a powerful country. It bordered Germany to the southwest. Hitler knew France would fight hard to prevent Germany from becoming too big and powerful. By the spring of 1940, Hitler was ready to go on the offensive again.

In April 1940, Germany invaded Denmark and Norway. One month later, the Battle of France began when Germany attacked Belgium, the Netherlands, and Luxembourg.

Between September 1939 and April 1940, French troops reinforced underground bunkers along their country's borders. Troops could travel through these bunkers on railroads.

These smaller countries would give German forces access to invade France.

The French had built a strong defensive system along the border between France and Germany. It was called the Maginot Line. But Hitler planned to surprise the French by invading France through the dense forests of Belgium. The Ardennes is a hilly forest that stretches from Belgium and Luxembourg into France. The French thought it would be impossible for German tanks to cross it.

But by 1940, Germany had developed new weapons. One was the panzer tank. It could roll quickly over uneven ground. German panzers rolled swiftly through the Ardennes into France. Starting on May 12, French and German forces fought for two days in the Battle of Sedan. Planes dropped bomb after bomb on French troops. French commanders ordered their soldiers to retreat and give up their ground. The Germans won the Battle of Sedan easily. But the Battle of France was not over.

THE BATTLE OF FRANCE

German tanks rolled through the Ardennes in Luxembourg, Belgium, and France starting on May 10, 1940. The map below shows the lines to which German troops had advanced throughout the month. How does this map help you understand Germany's invasion of France?

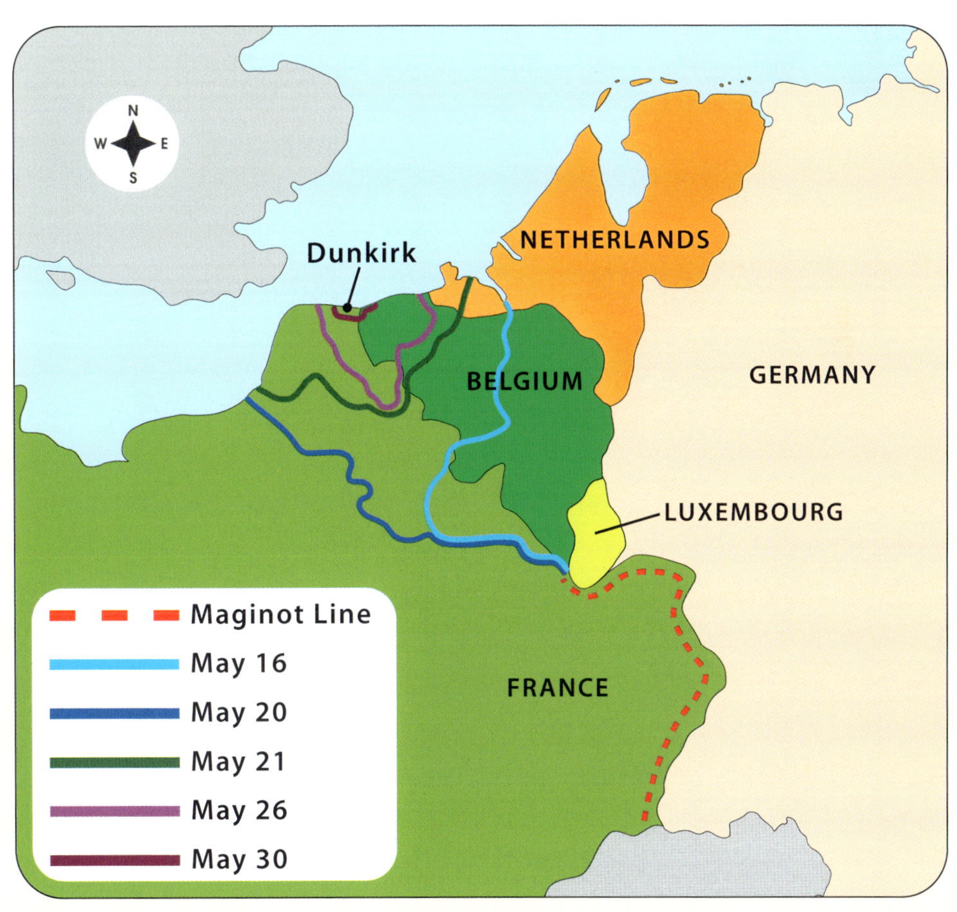

During the Dunkirk evacuation, troops lined up along the beach, waiting to be picked up by Allied ships.

DUNKIRK

By the last week of May, the German Army had reached the coast of northern France. They trapped Allied soldiers in an area around the port city of Dunkirk.

The only escape for these Allied troops was by sea. On the night of May 26, 1940, the British Royal Navy sent ships and hundreds of small boats to rescue soldiers from Dunkirk. The vessels carried more than 300,000 troops across the English Channel to southern England.

After the Dunkirk evacuation, the German Army moved south. Many German soldiers headed toward the French capital of Paris. Another German force attacked the Maginot Line from behind, on the French side. French fortresses fell one by one. The Germans marched into

PERSPECTIVES

THE DUNKIRK EVACUATION

Winston Churchill was the prime minister of Great Britain in 1940. He called the Dunkirk evacuation a miracle. He focused on the courage of those who rescued the troops. He said they never stopped in their mission even "under the ceaseless hail of bombs." His words changed Dunkirk from a retreat into a symbol of courage amid the Allies' defeat in France. This boosted the spirits of the British public.

French politician Philippe Pétain collaborated with the Nazi Party once Germany invaded France. He led the French government while the nation was under Germany's control.

Paris on June 14. France surrendered eight days later on June 22. The Germans took over northern France. The French were allowed to keep the southern half of their country, but Germany would control the new French government.

By the summer of 1940, the Allies had lost the Battle of France. Great Britain was the largest remaining Allied country left uninvaded by Germany. The country began to prepare for a German attack.

THE AXIS POWERS

Italy joined the war as Germany's ally on June 10, 1940. Benito Mussolini ruled Italy as a dictator. Mussolini had always supported the Nazi Party. He persecuted Italian Jews and punished Italians who spoke against his government. Mussolini also wanted to gain more land for Italy during the war.

FURTHER EVIDENCE

Chapter Two explains how Germany invaded France. What were some of the reasons why this invasion was successful? Go to the article below and watch the video about Hitler's fighting strategy. Does the information on the website present new evidence about Germany's success in France?

BLITZKRIEG EXPLAINED

abdocorelibrary.com/world-war-ii-europe

L1548
111
L1584
111
L1559
111

CHAPTER THREE

THE BATTLE OF BRITAIN

In the summer of 1940, Hitler made plans to invade Britain by sending troops across the English Channel. German soldiers and tanks would land on British soil and attack. The invasion plan was called Operation Sea Lion.

However, the British Royal Air Force (RAF) was strong. Hitler wanted to destroy the RAF before sending troops over water. German air attacks marked the beginning of the Battle of Britain.

The British Royal Air Force used many kinds of planes. The Hawker Hurricane was an important fighter plane in the Battle of Britain.

Radar operators used equipment to detect enemy aircraft. Radar technology showed where the aircraft were, which direction they were flying, and how many aircraft were approaching.

RADAR STATIONS

The RAF used radar stations to detect wireless communication and enemy planes up to 100 miles (160 km) away. Radar gave the RAF time to get its planes into the air to fight before German planes dropped bombs. A chain of radar stations stood along the coast of Britain. The German air force, called the Luftwaffe, bombed RAF radio stations on August 12, 1940. But they only knocked out one. The targets were difficult to hit.

Hermann Göring directed the Luftwaffe. Through the rest of August, he continued to send thousands of planes to bomb RAF airfields. Radar allowed the RAF to spot German planes, and the RAF took down more than 600 aircraft. But the British were running out of supplies.

THE BATTLE OF THE ATLANTIC

While Germany and Britain fought in the skies, the Battle of the Atlantic also raged in the ocean. This had been an ongoing struggle between Germany, Britain, and France throughout the war. During the fall of 1940, German submarines called U-boats increased their attacks against British trade ships. Germany tried to cut Britain's supply lines and force the country to surrender. Although the Germans failed to force Britain's surrender, the Battle of the Atlantic would continue for years to come.

THE BLITZ

On September 7, Hitler changed his strategy. German planes dropped bombs on the British city of London. This bombing campaign was called the Blitz. "Blitz" was short for *blitzkrieg*, or "lightning war." Every night, German planes dropped bombs on London. Hitler wanted to scare the British into surrendering. But the British would not surrender. The RAF fought back fiercely. On September 17, Hitler called off Operation Sea Lion. He knew if he sent his troops across the English Channel, the RAF would kill his men before they arrived on shore. But Germany continued to bomb London for months.

Meanwhile, on September 27, 1940, Japan joined the alliance between Germany and Italy. The three countries signed the Tripartite Pact. They became known as the Axis powers.

PERSPECTIVES

A COSTLY MISTAKE

Historians have debated why Britain won the Battle of Britain. Experts from York Saint John University believe one of Germany's key mistakes was not attacking more British airfields and destroying British radar systems. Instead the Luftwaffe turned its attention to bombing London. If Germany had focused solely on military targets such as radar stations, historians think Britain's chances of winning the battle would have been much worse.

STRAIGHT TO THE SOURCE

Winston Churchill gave a speech over British radio on June 18, 1940. Churchill was preparing his country for an attack from Germany. He said:

> *The whole fury and might of the enemy must very soon be turned on us. Hitler knows that he will have to break us in this island or lose the war. If we can stand up to him, all Europe may be free, and the life of the world may move forward into the broad, sunlit uplands. . . . But if we fail, then the whole world, including the United States, including all that we have known and cared for, will sink into the abyss of a new Dark Age. . . . Let us therefore brace ourselves to our duties . . . if the British Empire and Commonwealth last a thousand years, men will still say, "This was their finest hour."*

Source: "Their Finest Hour." *International Churchill Society*, n.d., winstonchurchill.org. Accessed 1 Nov. 2023.

WHAT'S THE BIG IDEA?

Read Churchill's speech carefully. What is Churchill's main idea in this speech? What words and phrases does he use to express his idea?

HITLER MOVES EAST

While German military generals were making plans to win new territory, Hitler was making changes in Germany and his conquered territory. The war brought more Jews under Nazi control. The Nazis moved forward with their plan to imprison and murder Jewish people. After the Nazis occupied Poland, they ordered all Polish Jews to live in Warsaw, in a settlement called a ghetto. The ghetto separated Jews from the rest of the population by a wall. Nazi and

Jewish people were enclosed behind a barbed wire fence in the Warsaw ghetto. Hundreds of thousands of people lived in an area of just 1.3 square miles (3.4 sq km).

Polish officers guarded the outside. Jews were sealed in on November 15, 1940. More than 400,000 Jews were imprisoned in the Warsaw ghetto. Tens of thousands of people died from disease and starvation.

The Warsaw ghetto was the largest Nazi ghetto, but it was not the only Nazi camp in German territory. The system would grow to include thousands of Nazi camps. At concentration camps, prisoners were forced to work under harsh conditions. At extermination camps, Nazis killed prisoners. Many sites used gas chambers. The Nazis and their collaborators deliberately murdered Jewish people, and their actions are known as the Holocaust. They also targeted other groups, such as the Roma people. Hitler's aim was to create a master race of white Germans with what he considered to be pure German blood.

OPERATION BARBAROSSA

By May 1941, Hitler realized the British were not going to give up. Hitler turned his attention to his next target:

Soviet troops fought back against the Germans in Leningrad.

the Soviet Union. Soviet leader Joseph Stalin thought he was safe from a German invasion. But Stalin had seized new territories since 1939. Hitler did not like that. He wanted to conquer all of Europe himself. Hitler turned on Stalin, and the German invasion of the Soviet Union began on June 22, 1941. It was called Operation Barbarossa. The Soviet Union joined the Allies after Germany began its attack.

German forces and their allies surrounded the city of Leningrad in September 1941. Leningrad was an important city to capture. It was a main port for bringing goods into the Soviet Union. By capturing Leningrad, Germans would cut off valuable supplies for the Soviets. But the people of Leningrad would not surrender.

Meanwhile, another German unit headed to the Soviet capital of Moscow, where Stalin had his headquarters. The German forces got stuck outside Moscow in October 1941 because of bad weather. They could hardly advance. On December 5, 1941, the Soviets launched a counterattack. The Germans were forced to retreat.

PERSPECTIVES

A COLD WINTER

Hitler blamed the weather for the failure of Operation Barbarossa. German troops did not have enough fuel or supplies. They had not been prepared for winter warfare. But historians think there were many reasons Germany was defeated in the Soviet Union. Hitler had been overly confident he could win. He thought the war would be short. He had not planned for a long campaign. Hitler had not understood that the Soviets would fight back so hard.

THE UNITED STATES ENTERS THE WAR

While Hitler was fighting the Soviet Union, new alliances formed. On December 7, 1941, Japan attacked the US military base at Pearl Harbor in Hawaii. On December 8, the United States declared war on Japan. Italy and Germany quickly came to the aid of their ally and declared war on the United States.

World War II was now a global war. The United States prepared to enter the conflict. The first US troops arrived in the British Isles in January 1942.

In August 1942, German forces reached the Soviet city of Stalingrad. The Germans bombed the city into rubble, and then they moved in and took control. But the citizens of Stalingrad would not give up. They hid all over the city. They fought Germans in the streets and from the sewers. By November 1942, the Soviet Union's Red Army had circled the city and trapped the German troops inside. The Germans quickly ran out of food and bullets. They surrendered on February 2, 1943.

"RAT WAR"

After German troops moved into Stalingrad, Soviet soldiers hid in factories, house basements, and sewers. They fought back using bayonets, homemade exploding devices, and daggers. The two sides fought each other in the streets for every inch of territory. The Germans called this kind of fighting "rat war." The Germans were surprised by Soviet fighters popping up in unexpected places.

The German defeat in the Battle of Stalingrad was a turning point in the war in Europe. About 40,000 Soviet citizens and more than 1 million Soviet soldiers died or were injured in Stalingrad alone. Meanwhile, an estimated 1.5 million Axis fighters were killed, wounded, or captured. Hitler and his forces were starting to weaken. The Battle of Stalingrad was the first large-scale loss suffered by the Germans in the war.

The Siege of Leningrad ended almost one year later, on January 27, 1944. After nearly 900 days, the Red Army drove German forces away. Almost 1 million Leningrad residents had died during the siege.

STRAIGHT TO THE SOURCE

A survivor of the Battle of Stalingrad described what it was like when the Germans first attacked. He said:

> *[German planes] swooped down on the river station, dropping bombs and shooting with their machine guns. The pilots must have been able to see that all the people on the riverbank were civilians. But they were acting like professional assassins. They opened fire on [defenseless] women and children, and chose their targets so as to kill the maximum number of people. They dropped their bombs on the crowds just as the people were beginning to get on the ferries. . . . People tried to make the crossing not only on ferries and barges. They went on overloaded rowing boats, even on logs and barrels or planks lashed together with wire. And the Nazis opened fire from the air on everything that floated. It was like a hunt.*

Source: Jonathan Bastable. *Notes from Stalingrad.* Greenhill Books, 2019, pp. 46–47.

BACK IT UP

The author of this passage is using evidence to support a point. Write a paragraph describing the point the author is making. Then write down two or three pieces of evidence the author uses to make the point.

CHAPTER FIVE

PATH TO VICTORY

In July 1943, the Italian government removed Benito Mussolini from power. A new leader named Pietro Badoglio was chosen. Badoglio spoke out against Italy's alliance with Hitler. Badoglio arranged a secret truce with the Allies, which was announced on September 8, 1943. But Germany refused to give up. Allied and German forces were already stationed in Italy. German troops quickly seized two-thirds of the country. Fighting between Germany and the Allies continued in Italy until the war's end in 1945.

Italian and Allied leaders signed an armistice on September 3, 1943. This agreement was a truce between Italian and Allied forces.

Hundreds of thousands of reinforcements arrived in Normandy after the initial invasion on June 6, 1944.

THE BATTLE OF NORMANDY

By the end of May 1944, there were more than 1.5 million US troops in Britain. They had arrived to take part in an Allied invasion of northern France. Operation Overlord was the Allies' plan to invade Normandy, France. If they succeeded, Allied troops would fight to free the rest of northwest Europe from Germany. The Normandy Invasion was also called D-Day.

In the early morning hours of June 6, 1944, more than 150,000 Allied troops landed on the beaches of Normandy. Over the next few weeks, Allied forces fought their way across the Normandy countryside. By the end of August, they had reached Paris. The Allies freed the city on August 25, 1945. The Normandy Invasion turned the tide of war against the Nazis. Hitler was now fighting Soviet forces from the east and Allied forces from the west. His army was growing weaker with the loss of men and weapons.

LIBERATING NAZI CAMPS

As the Red Army closed in from the east, Germans began to move Nazi camp prisoners away from the front lines of fighting. The Nazis wanted to cover up their murder of Jews. In the winter of 1944 to 1945, the Germans marched tens of thousands of prisoners out of camps. These journeys were called death marches. Many prisoners died or were killed along the way. The Nazis also destroyed the camps' gas chambers.

As Allied forces moved across Europe, they found Nazi camps that Germany hadn't hidden. Survivors in the camps were sick and starving. The Red Army had freed a camp called Majdanek in Poland on July 23, 1943. It was the first Nazi camp to be liberated. Allied troops continued to free prisoners from camps in 1944 and 1945. The world soon learned details about the Nazi's crimes against Jews and other groups.

THE FINAL BATTLES

In December 1944, Hitler tried one last counterattack to regain territory. The Battle of the Bulge began on December 16. German forces surprised Allied soldiers in the Ardennes Forest. The Germans attacked in snowy weather. The bad weather prevented the Allies from getting any air support for three days. Germans pushed their way into Belgium and Luxembourg. The battle line began to look like a bulge on the map. But when the weather cleared in January, more Allied help arrived. The Germans were forced back into Germany. Losing the Battle of the Bulge left Germany with few troops or supplies.

Hitler went into hiding in his underground bunker on January 16, 1945. The bunker was in the German capital of Berlin. In March, US bomber planes attacked Berlin. On April 21, the Red Army entered Berlin, beginning the Battle of Berlin. By April 30, the Red Army reached the center of the city. Hitler could hear the sounds of battle getting closer. He refused to be taken prisoner. He took his own life on April 30, 1945.

PERSPECTIVES

BOMBING OF DRESDEN

From February 13 to 15, 1945, Allied forces bombed Dresden, Germany. Historians estimate that between 25,000 and 35,000 civilians were killed, and much of the city was destroyed. Some Allied leaders believed these attacks were necessary. RAF air marshal Arthur Harris wrote, "Attacks on cities . . . are strategically justified in so far as they tend to shorten the war and preserve the lives of Allied soldiers." However, other leaders questioned the morality of this attack.

THE WAR'S END

After the Battle of Berlin, Germany agreed

to an unconditional surrender. A German commander signed surrender documents in France on May 7, 1945. The next day, another officer signed surrender documents between Germany and the Soviet Union. Germany's surrender marked an Allied victory in Europe.

Fighting in the Pacific would last for another four months. Japan surrendered after the United States dropped two atomic bombs on the Japanese cities of Hiroshima and Nagasaki on August 6 and 9. Japan announced its surrender on August 15. World War II officially ended on September 2, 1945, after Japan signed documents of surrender.

World War II was the deadliest conflict in recorded history.

HITLER'S BUNKER

Hitler built an underground hiding place in 1944. It was his final headquarters in the last months of World War II in Europe. The complex had a concrete roof that was more than 10 feet (3 m) thick. His hideaway was made of two bunkers connected by a guarded staircase. There were about 30 rooms in all.

WORLD WAR II DEATHS BY COUNTRY

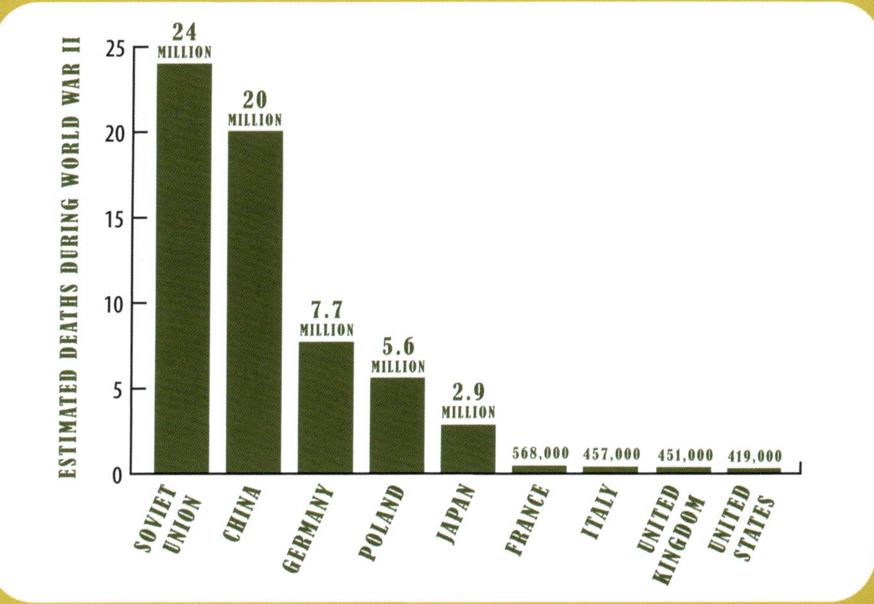

This graph shows an estimate of how many people died from a few major countries during World War II. Why might some countries have had higher death tolls than others? Which country had the highest death toll? What might explain that answer?

No one is sure exactly how many people died during the war. Some estimates say 60 million people or more died. About 15 to 20 million of those people died in Europe. At least 6 million Jewish people died during the Holocaust. Nazis also killed hundreds of thousands of people from other persecuted groups. It would take decades before the world recovered from the conflict.

IMPORTANT DATES

September 1, 1939
World War II officially begins when Germany invades Poland. Great Britain and France declare war on Germany two days later.

May 10, 1940
The Battle of France begins.

September 27, 1940
Japan joins the alliance between Germany and Italy. The countries become known as the Axis powers.

December 7, 1941
Japanese planes bomb the US military base at Pearl Harbor. The United States enters the war to fight alongside the Allied forces the following day.

September 8, 1943
Italy and the Allied powers officially announce a truce.

June 6, 1944
The Allies storm the beaches of Normandy, France, forcing the Germans to fight on two fronts.

December 16, 1944
The Germans launch a surprise attack on the Allies at the Battle of the Bulge. It is not successful, and the German forces retreat.

April 30, 1945
Berlin is surrounded, and Adolf Hitler ends his life.

May 7, 1945
Germany surrenders, ending the war in Europe.

September 2, 1945
The Allies accept Japan's surrender. World War II officially ends.

STOP AND THINK

Tell the Tale

Chapter One of this book discusses what Polish citizens experienced when the Germans invaded. Imagine you were there. Write 200 words about what you see and how you feel when your city is under attack.

Surprise Me

Chapter Three discusses the Battle of Britain. After reading this chapter, what two or three facts about the battle did you find most surprising? Write a few sentences about each fact. Why did you find each fact surprising?

Take a Stand

Many European countries went through sieges during World War II. Warsaw, Leningrad, and Stalingrad were cities under German sieges that lasted many months. Some citizens tried to escape. Other citizens hid and fought back. Do you think it is better to try to flee or to fight when enemies attack? Explain why. What things do you consider when making your decision?

Another View

Chapter Two talks about the rescue at Dunkirk. As you know, every source is different. Ask a librarian or another adult to help you find another source about this event. Write a short essay comparing and contrasting the new source's point of view with that of this book's author. What is the point of view of each author? How are they similar and why? How are they different and why?

GLOSSARY

anti-Semitic
discriminating against Jewish people

civilian
a person who is not in the military

dictator
a ruler who rules by force and has total power over a country

empire
a group of countries or territories ruled by one leader or government

extermination
complete destruction, usually of a whole group

genocide
the deliberate killing of a large number of people from a nation or ethnic group

nationalistic
relating to the belief that one nation is better than others and other nations should be more like it

persecuted
punished or harmed because of political beliefs

radar
a system used to detect the location of objects such as aircraft

siege
an attack that surrounds a place and cuts it off from help or supplies

ONLINE RESOURCES

To learn more about World War II in Europe, visit our free resource websites below.

Visit **abdocorelibrary.com** or scan this QR code for free Common Core resources for teachers and students, including vetted activities, multimedia, and booklinks, for deeper subject comprehension.

Visit **abdobooklinks.com** or scan this QR code for free additional online weblinks for further learning. These links are routinely monitored and updated to provide the most current information available.

LEARN MORE

Hearn, Hattie. *Tales of World War II*. Neon Squid, 2023.

Hudak, Heather C. *Causes of World War II*. Abdo, 2025.

World War II. DK, 2021.

INDEX

About the Author

Janie Havemeyer is the author of many books for young readers. Janie lives in San Francisco, California. When Janie is not writing, she likes to read about history, spend time with her family, and travel. Her father was a lieutenant in the US Army and served in the Pacific.